TAKE A PICTURE OF ME, JAMES VANDERZEE!

BY ANDREA J. LONEY

ILLUSTRATED BY KEITH MALLETT

Lee & Low Books Inc.
New York

ACKNOWLEDGMENTS

Thanks to my amazing editorial fairy godmother, Jessica Echeverria; my mom, Phyllis Slaten; early readers Johan Beckles and Kathy Halsey; critique partners Cate Williams, Cheryl Kim, Frances Kalavritinos, Glenn Hanna, Suzanne Harris, and Zeena Pliska; PB sherpas Glenda Armand, Irene Fertik, Sheri Fink, Susan J. Berger, and Sylvia Liu, and for the love and support of Christopher, Dorothy, and John Schwarz. So grateful to 12x12, SCBWI-LA, Children's Book Writers of Los Angeles, and the Los Angeles Public Library. Many thanks also to Donna Mussenden VanDerZee for helping us share her beloved husband's story with the world.

LEE & LOW BOOKS Inc., 95 Madison Avenue, New York, NY 10016
leeandlow.com
Book design by Ashley Halsey
Book production by The Kids at Our House
The text is set in Archer
The illustrations are rendered in acrylic on canvas
Manufactured in China by First Choice Printing Co. Ltd., May 2017
Printed on paper from responsible sources
10 9 8 7 6 5 4 3 2 1
First Edition
Library of Congress Cataloging–in–Publication Data
Names: Loney, Andrea J., author. | Mallett, Keith, illustrator.
Title: Take a picture of me, James VanDerZee! / by Andrea J. Loney; illustrated by Keith Mallett.
Description: First edition. | New York, NY: Lee & Low Books Inc., 2017. |
Audience: Ages 7-11.
Identifiers: LCCN 2016048140 | ISBN 9781620142608 (hardcover: alk. paper)
Subjects: LCSH: Van Der Zee, James, 1886-1983. | Photographers—United States—Biography—Juvenile literature. | African American photographers—New York (State)—New York—Biography—Juvenile literature. | Harlem Renaissance—Juvenile literature.
Classification: LCC TR140.V37 L66 2017 | DDC 770.92 [B]—dc23
LC record available at https://lccn.loc.gov/2016048140

For Grandpa Harvey, the classical pianist,
and Granddaddy Aston, the picture-takin' man—A.J.L.

To my mom, Dorothy—K.M.

Deep in the heart of Lenox, Massachusetts,
in a white frame house nestled between his aunts' home
and his grandparents' house,
lived a boy named James VanDerZee.

James was the oldest boy
of three sons and two daughters.
At the VanDerZee's, the children learned
about music and art,
and kindness too.

James played the violin and piano.
He also liked to paint,
but drawing people was hard.
He could never get their expressions right.
James wanted to share the beauty
he saw in his heart.

One day a man came to the VanDerZee home
with a huge contraption called a camera.
It was the only camera in Lenox.
Click! Boom!
The man took the family's picture and left.

Later he returned with a photograph
that perfectly captured everyone's smiles
and their mother's sweet gaze.
Now this is how you make great pictures,
thought James. *I want a camera.*

In a magazine, James found a contest
where the first prize was a camera.
To win, he had to sell
the most sachets of ladies' perfume.
After months of selling sachets,
James won! He won!
But the camera came in parts,
and the parts didn't fit together.
So James had to start over again.
He weeded his neighbor's garden
for a quarter a day until he saved five dollars.
And then, James was the second person
in Lenox to own a camera.

First James took pictures of his family.

Then his classmates.

Soon people from all over town were saying,

"Take a picture of me, James VanDerZee!"

At home James turned his closet into a darkroom
and learned how to develop film.
It wasn't easy to create photographs,
but James loved his family.
He loved his town and the people in it.
So he always worked to make them look their best.

Far away from Lenox, the world was changing.
Many black families were leaving
the segregated South to start new lives
in big northern towns like New York City.
James was ready for an adventure.
At the age of eighteen, he took his camera
and moved to Harlem.
Whoo!
Compared to Lenox,
Harlem was big, fast, and exciting.
James had to hold on to his hat
to keep his head from spinning.

After working as a pianist, a waiter,
and an elevator operator,
James finally got a job as an assistant photographer
at a portrait studio in New Jersey.
Many big-city customers came
to have their portraits taken.
James couldn't wait to take their photographs,
but his boss sent him straight to the darkroom.
He said customers would not want
their portraits taken by a black man.

James did not like the way
his boss took portraits.
His boss shot the photographs too quickly.
Sometimes the customers
weren't even ready.

In the darkroom, James worked hard
to make everyone look their best.
One day his boss left for vacation
and put James in charge of the shop.
James promised to take care of the business . . .
but in his own way.

Instead of rushing the customers,
James talked to them.
He found their natural smiles
and the perfect backgrounds.
James treated the customers
like family.

In the darkroom,
James made their pictures look even better.
He brightened people's eyes,
straightened their teeth,
and fixed their hair.
He saw what was special in everyone
and captured each person's story on film.

When James's boss returned
he found a line of customers saying,
"Take a picture of me, James VanDerZee!"
So James went back to New York
and opened his very own portrait studio in Harlem,
where the neighborhood was jumping
with brand-new music, art,
books, and glamour.
This cultural celebration was called
the Harlem Renaissance.

W. 125 ST.

LENOX

Just about everyone—
politicians like Marcus Garvey,
athletes like Joe Louis and
the New York Black Yankees,
and world-famous performers
like Florence Mills,
Bill "Bojangles" Robinson,
and Mamie Smith—
wanted fancy portraits taken
by James VanDerZee.

James photographed the rich and the poor,
but mostly the middle class.
And this distinguished him
from many other photographers.
At the time, photographs of black people
were often sad and grim depictions
of poor farm workers
or struggling city dwellers.
But when James stepped behind the camera,
Click! Boom!
Everything changed.

James used beautiful backgrounds,
fancy props, and elegant clothing
to help the people of his neighborhood
look their best.
In the darkroom he fixed photos
and combined images
to create perfect portraits.

Even James's street photography
captured the pride, beauty, and joy of Harlem.
People all over the world
proudly displayed James's photos
in their homes, in their businesses,
and close to their hearts.

But the world was changing again.

Cameras were now smaller and cheaper.

People could take their own photographs.

Soon customers stopped coming

to James VanDerZee's studio.

James tried to keep working.
He took passport photos,
shooting tiny portraits
that helped send folks on faraway adventures.
Eventually, though, James had no choice
but to put away his camera.
Instead he fixed up old photographs
sent to him by people from around the world.

Several years later, a visitor arrived
at James's studio.
The Metropolitan Museum of Art
needed photographs for an exhibit
on the history of Harlem.
They found thousands of photos,
showing thousands of Harlem residents—
all taken by James VanDerZee.

The exhibit was called *Harlem on My Mind,*
and James's work was a huge hit!
People said it was like walking
through forty years
of the history of Harlem.

The photographs showed the Harlem
of families and churches, friends and clubs,
neighbors and celebrities.
The Harlem of love, pride, and community.
The Harlem that James VanDerZee
always saw in his heart.
And people came to say,
"Take a picture of me, James VanDerZee!"
So James stepped behind the camera once again.
Click! Click!

AFTERWORD

In 1884, John and Susan Elizabeth VanDerZee, the butler and maid for President Ulysses S. Grant, left their posts in his New York residence to start a family. They moved to Lenox, Massachusetts, a sleepy, multicultural town that became a vacation retreat for wealthy aristocrats in the summer. A year after their first child, Jennie, arrived, James Augustus Joseph VanDerZee was born on June 29, 1886. The next year their son Walter was born, and three more children, Charles, Johnny (who died at age six), and Mary, followed.

James's first working camera was a four-by-five-inch box camera, operated on a stand. With supplies from the local drugstore, he developed his own pictures by following the directions that came with his first camera—the broken one. James was only a fifth grader when he became his school's photographer. He was also the unofficial town photographer, and even took portraits of vacationing aristocrats.

Eventually, James outgrew life in his small town. In 1904, eighteen-year-old James and his brother Walter decided to join their father, who was working as a waiter at the Knickerbocker Trust in New York City. James took on many jobs. He played the violin and piano with the

James VanDerZee, Lenox, Massachusetts, c. 1900

Interior, G.G.G. Photo Studio, 1930

Fletcher Henderson and John Wanamaker Orchestras. In 1911, James got a job as an assistant photographer in a portrait studio in Newark, New Jersey. The next year he joined his sister Jennie at the Toussaint Conservatory of Art and Music, where James photographed her young students. He honed his craft there until 1915, when James opened the Guarantee Photo Studio at 109 West 135th Street in Harlem with his new business partner, Gaynella Greenlee. Then they moved to a better location—the renamed G.G.G. Photo Studio, located at 272 Lenox Avenue. James and Gaynella were married for more than fifty years.

From 1915 through the 1980s, James took pictures of families, churches, businesses, soldiers, professional organizations, performers, athletes, religious leaders, and more. Marcus Garvey's "Back to Africa" movement, the Universal Negro Improvement Association, hired James as the organization's official photographer.

Couple in Raccoon Coats, 1932

Eventually, once cameras became smaller, cheaper, and easier to use, James's business declined. He went through hard times— losing his home, his wife Gaynella, and even the rights to his own photographs. Then, in 1978, he married Donna Mussenden, and everything changed. With his new wife's encouragement and support, James regained the rights to his work, returned to his career, and started taking pictures again. James created portraits for many celebrities, including Jean-Michel Basquiat, Lou Rawls, and Muhammad Ali.

Donna Mussenden VanDerZee, 1982.

Alpha Phi Alpha Basketball team, 1926

James VanDerZee saw himself as an artist first, then a photographer. He was a master at transforming simple photographs into elaborate works of art. The camera was only one part of a complete set of tools he used to create portraits. First came the special lighting, clothing, backgrounds, and props. Second, James's humor and warmth helped his customers relax for the camera.

Finally, after the pictures were taken, James used a couple of techniques to perfect the portraits in the darkroom. He used an etching knife and a retouching pencil to erase parts of images, such as wrinkles, or draw in "corrections," such as straight teeth. Sometimes he even brightened the subject's eyes and smile, as in the portrait below.

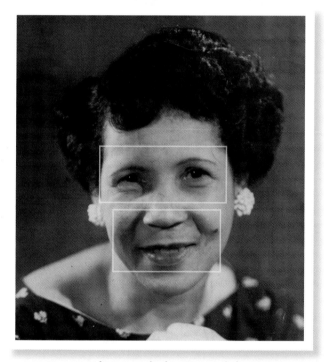

Portrait of Woman before Retouching, c. 1930

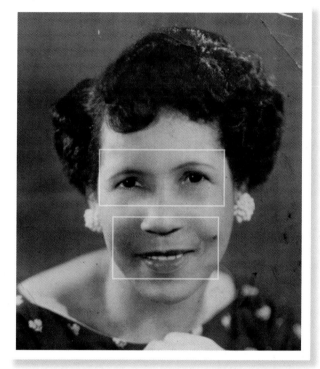

Portrait of Woman after Retouching, c. 1930

James also mastered the art of photomontage. This technique allowed him to take two or more pictures and then combine them into one final image. Sometimes he would show only a partial layer of an image, which would make the people in the photo seem transparent, as if they were spirits or angels. In *Future Expectations*, the photo below, James used this technique to show a newly married couple's wish to have a family.

Future Expectations, 1926

Chocolate Soda Wagon, 1928

During his lifetime James VanDerZee created thousands of portraits, took more than 75,000 photographs, and created more than 125,000 plates, negatives, transparencies, and prints. Each image shared an extraordinary story about the people of Harlem, the quiet beauty of their everyday lives, the grandeur of their hopes and dreams, and most of all, their inherent dignity and pride. James passed away in 1983 at the age of ninety-six.

After the life and work of James VanDerZee, the world has never seen Harlem in quite the same way.

Daddy's Girl, 1937

James VanDerZee's likeness and the following photographs were used as models for illustrations in the book:

cover: *James VanDerZee, self-portrait*, 1918.
p. 23: *Joe Louis, Champion Boxer*, c. 1930; *Marcus Garvey in Regalia*, 1924;
  Florence Mills, 1927; *New York Black Yankees (Negro League)*, 1934;
  Bill "Bojangles" Robinson, Actor/Tap Dancer, c. 1920;
  and *Mamie Smith, Blues Singer*, c. 1923.
pp. 24, 29, and 31: *Couple in Raccoon Coats*, 1932.
pp. 22, 29, and 30: *Stylish Harlem Couple*, c. 1930.
pp. 26 and 31: *Bride and Groom*, 1937.
p. 31: *Cousin Susan Porter*, c. 1915; *UNIA Protest
  Parade*, 1924.
pp. 31 and 33: *Family Portrait*, c. 1940.
pp. 33: *Star Performance*, c. 1930; *Dance Class*, 1928;
  Jean-Michel Basquiat, 1982, and *James VanDerZee, 1980*

BIBLIOGRAPHY

Haskins, Jim. *James Van DerZee: The Picture Takin' Man*. New York: Dodd, Mead, 1979.
Legacy of James Van Der Zee: A Portrait of Black Americans, The. New York: Alternative Center for International Arts, 1977. Exhibition catalog.
Van Der Zee, James, Owen Dodson, and Camille Billops. *The Harlem Book of the Dead*. Dobbs Ferry, NY: Morgan & Morgan, 1978.
Willis, Deborah. *Reflections in Black: A History of Black Photographers, 1840 to the Present*. New York: W. W. Norton, 2000.
Willis-Braithwaite, Deborah. *VanDerZee, Photographer, 1886–1983*. New York: Harry N. Abrams, 1993.

FOR FURTHER READING

De Cock, Liliane and Reginald McGhee, eds. *James Van DerZee*. Dobbs Ferry, NY: Morgan & Morgan, 1973.
McGhee, Reginald. *The World of James Van DerZee: A Visual Record of Black Americans*. New York: Grove Press, 1969.
Mercer, Kobena. *James VanDerZee*. London and New York: Phaidon, 2003.
Roots in Harlem: Photographs by James VanDerZee, from the Collection of Regenia A. Perry. Memphis, TN: Memphis Memorial Art Gallery, 1989. Exhibition catalog.